ECHOES
INVISIBLE

A. J Schneider

Dedication

To everyone who has navigated the shadows of sadness, loneliness, and abandonment, and to those who have felt that hope has slipped away: this book is for you. May it serve as a beacon, guiding you to the profound realization of your innate worth and purpose. You are, unequivocally, enough.

In the words of Scripture, ***"I can do all things through Christ who strengthens me." - Philippians 4:13.*** This verse echoes the heart of this book: in the midst of our trials, we are never alone and always enough.

Table Of Contents

Chapter 1: Invisible Lines

Alex walked through the crowded hallways feeling invisible. Each step was a reminder that he didn't fit in, that he was different. The vibrant laughter and animated chatter around him only emphasized the silence that cloaked his presence. He moved like a ghost, unseen and unheard, his difference a barrier that seemed impossible.

It wasn't just his interests or his style that set him apart—it was something deeper, something he couldn't change even if he tried. Alex often caught glimpses of his reflection in the school's windows, wondering if there was something inherently wrong with him, something that made him unworthy of attention, of friendship, of love.

As he sat in the back of the classroom, he felt the weight of loneliness pressing down on him. Teachers' voices became a distant echo as his mind wandered. He pondered if God saw him, if He cared. Alex struggled with the notion that maybe he was just as invisible to God as he was to his peers.

He found solace in the verses of Psalm 139, where it was written that God had seen him even before he was born. It spoke of a God who knew him intimately, who had crafted him purposefully. "But why," Alex thought, "would such a God allow him to feel so utterly alone?"

The bell rang, pulling him back to reality. He gathered his books and headed to his next class, a silent prayer in his heart that somehow, he would find a way to bridge the gap between himself and the world.

Alex's days followed a monotonous and painful pattern. Each morning he awoke to the sound of his alarm, a shrill reminder that another day of struggle lay ahead. He'd drag himself out of bed, his reflection in the mirror doing nothing to lift the weight of dread that settled in his stomach.

Breakfast was a silent affair. His parents were always too caught up in their own routines to notice the clouds of despair that hung over him. They didn't see the way his hands shook slightly as he held his spoon or the way he pushed his food around the plate, appetite lost to anxiety.

At school, the hallways felt like a gauntlet. With his head down, he navigated through groups of students, each cluster a fortress of familiarity he couldn't penetrate. Their easy laughter felt like a language he couldn't speak, their casual touches and shared glances a country for which he had no visa.

During lunch, the library became his sanctuary. The books were his silent, steadfast friends, offering worlds he could escape into, lives more thrilling and happier than his own. But even between the pages of his favorite novels, he couldn't fully evade the pervasive feeling of being an outsider.

In the solitude of the library, Alex would often flip through the worn pages of his pocket Bible, the edges frayed from use. The words of Psalm 139:15-16

" My frame was not hidden from you when I was made in the secret place, when I was woven together in the depths of the earth. Your eyes saw my unformed body; all the days ordained for me were written in your book before one of them came to be."

whispered a comforting truth, that he was known. Yet, this knowledge was a double-edged sword, for if he was known so completely, why was he left to face this loneliness?

The afternoons were a blur of classes where he felt more like a ghost than a participant. Group projects were a nightmare, as he was always the last to be chosen, the one whose ideas were overlooked or dismissed. He began to doubt his worth, his capability, and even his existence.

At home, the silence of his room was a stark contrast to the chaos of school. Here, he was alone with his thoughts, which were often darker than the dimming light outside his window. He wondered if anyone would notice if he just stopped showing up, stopped trying to be part of a world that seemed to have no place for him.

As night fell, he'd lie in bed staring at the ceiling, the shadows cast by the streetlights playing over the walls. The darkness outside mirrored the one within, a cavernous, unfillable void. He yearned for sleep, for in sleep, he wasn't the odd one out, the misfit. In dreams, he was just Alex, and that was enough.

The Scripture's assurances felt distant, like a faint radio signal he strained to hear over the static of his life. "You are fearfully and wonderfully made..." the verse went, but fear was all Alex felt, a fear that he might never find his place, that the invisible lines that marked him as different might never be erased.

He clung to the promises of the Bible as a lifeline in a sea of doubt. The belief that he was made in the image of God was a raft he held onto, even as the waves of despair threatened to pull him under. In his most honest moments, he admitted to himself that he didn't just want to be seen by God; he wanted to be seen by someone with skin on, someone in the halls, in the classes, at home.

As the world slept, Alex wrestled with his thoughts, with his prayers, with the very essence of who he was. In the quiet of the night, the invisible lines felt all too tangible, like walls closing in. But somewhere deep inside, a stubborn spark of hope refused to be extinguished. He would face another day, another battle. And maybe, just maybe, he would find a way to connect, to be seen, to be known not just by God, but by those around him.

And so, with a heavy heart but a glimmer of hope, he drifted into a fitful sleep, the silent prayer from his heart carrying into the dreams that awaited him.

Chapter 2: Shadows in the Hallway

As the days turned into weeks, and weeks into months, the shadows in the hallway grew longer and darker for Alex. Laughter and light seemed to shrink away whenever he approached, and the isolation became suffocating. The more he felt the sting of exclusion, the more he retreated into himself, finding solace in the only thing that seemed to blur the harsh lines of his reality—drugs.

The drugs whispered promises of oblivion, a sweet escape from the pain of his existence. They were his companions in the lonely nights, his refuge from the piercing stares and whispered judgments. They didn't care that he was different; they didn't ask him to change.

But even as he sought comfort in their numbing embrace, a part of Alex ached for something more, something real. He couldn't shake the feeling of despair, the sense that he was walking through the darkest valley, as the Psalmist wrote. Yet, in the depths of his heart, a small flame of hope flickered weakly—the words of Psalm 23 promised that he was not alone, that there was a shepherd who walked with him, who held a rod and a staff to comfort him.

On a particularly difficult night, when the shadows seemed to close in around him, Alex reached for his Bible instead of the drugs. His hands trembled as he read the familiar verses, allowing the words to wash over him, to fill the room with a presence he couldn't see but desperately hoped was there.

"Even though I walk through the darkest valley, I will fear no evil, for you are with me." The words echoed in his mind as sleep finally claimed him, the drugs lying untouched on the nightstand, and for the first time in a long time, his dreams were not of darkness, but of a light guiding him home.

Alex's retreat into the corners of the school's corridors was a retreat into himself, where the echoes of his thoughts were his constant companions. The shadows cast by the lockers became his confidants, hiding his presence from the indifferent faces passing by. Each day melded into the next, a monochrome blur of monotony and whispered self-doubts.

In these hallways, where the flicker of fluorescent lights did little to warm the coldness he felt inside, Alex discovered a dangerous escape. The drugs were easy to come by, a whispered offer in a dimly lit bathroom, a quick exchange behind the gym. They promised solace, a numbing of the acute pain that came from being so profoundly disconnected from those around him. And for a while, they delivered.

When the high set in, the sharp edges of his world softened. The laughter that seemed to mock him now floated by, meaningless. The invitations to gatherings that never came now mattered less. In his chemically induced haze, Alex could almost convince himself that the loneliness was bearable, that the ache in his chest was just a temporary affliction.

But as the effects waned, the reality of his isolation became more pronounced. The shadows grew darker, the silence louder. The Scripture he once found comforting now haunted him. "Even though I walk through the darkest valley," the psalmist had written. But where was the comfort of the staff, the guidance of the rod? Why did every step feel more like a stumble deeper into despair?

In the moments when the artificial euphoria slipped away, Alex's heart yearned for something real, something lasting. He would lean against the cool metal of the lockers, closing his eyes, and whisper the psalm under his breath, a plea for it to be true. "I will fear no evil, for you are with me," he would say, hoping to feel the truth of those words, to sense the presence of the Shepherd that was promised to be there.

But each whispered prayer seemed to vanish into the void, and Alex was left feeling more abandoned than before. The cycle of highs and lows became his reality, the shadows in the hallway growing longer with each passing day, reaching out like fingers trying to pull him further into the darkness.

And so the battle raged within him, between the fleeting comfort of his escape and the deep-seated longing for a reprieve that was true and pure. In the lonely corridors of his heart and his school, Alex walked on, enveloped by shadows, searching for a light that seemed just out of reach.

Chapter 3: The Brink of Despair

The world seemed to spin a little slower for Alex as he walked through the schoolyard, the echoes of his past whispering in the wind. He could almost hear the innocent laughter of his younger self, playing without worry, without the heavy cloak of invisibility that now shrouded him. Back then, his differences were sources of pride, unique colors in the tapestry of his being. But those colors had faded, washed out by the stark reality of adolescence.

With each step, memories flickered in his mind like old film reels—birthday parties where he was the hero, school projects that earned him praise, the warm embrace of his grandmother telling him he was destined for greatness. These fragments of a happier time were now just ghosts, haunting the hollow spaces between his heartbeats.

Homework and grades, once a source of accomplishment, had lost their luster.

Alex's report card was a map of a terrain he no longer navigated with ease. The red marks and scribbled notes from teachers were just another confirmation of his gradual descent.

At home, the situation was no better. His parents' worried glances and hushed conversations pierced him with a mixture of guilt and resentment. They tiptoed around him, as if he were made of glass, ready to shatter at the slightest touch. The distance between them grew with each passing day, measured in missed dinners and unasked questions.

In the privacy of his room, Alex would often open the old family album, tracing the lines of his own smile with a trembling finger, wondering where that joy had gone. The Scriptures his grandmother had lovingly noted in the margins, verses of hope and promises of God's faithfulness, now seemed like words from another lifetime.

It was in these quiet moments of reflection that the pain cut the deepest. The contrast between what was and what is served as a cruel reminder of all that had been lost. The Bible lay on his nightstand, its leather cover worn from use. Sometimes, he would open it to Proverbs 14:13, which read, "Even in laughter the heart may ache, and rejoicing may end in grief." The truth of it resonated within him, a somber melody in the symphony of his sorrow.

Yet, even as he grappled with the traces of his past, Alex could not shake the feeling that there was something more, a purpose he was meant to find, a path he was destined to walk. The whispers of the past, for all their melancholy, seemed to be pushing him towards a future he could not yet see. It was this sliver of hope, thin and fragile, that kept the total darkness at bay.

As the sun set and the shadows lengthened, Alex closed the album and turned off the light. He lay in bed, the whispers of the past a lullaby that carried him into a restless sleep, where dreams and reality blurred in the dance of what was, what is, and what could still be.

Alex's room was his sanctuary, a small universe where he could be himself without the masks and pretenses that the world demanded. The walls, once adorned with posters of superheroes and athletes, now bore the marks of a mind in turmoil — sketches of shadows, eyes that seemed to look right through you, and a single, fading photograph of himself as a child, smiling without a care in the world.

That night, as he lay in bed surrounded by the silence of his room, Alex's thoughts turned to the moments that used to bring him joy. He remembered the rush of scoring a goal on the soccer field, the satisfaction of acing a test, the warmth of his friends' laughter. These memories, though faded, were like stars in the night sky — distant, yet still offering a glimmer of light.

The Bible his grandmother had given him was a constant presence. It was a connection to her, a thread that linked him to a time when faith seemed as natural as breathing. He remembered how she would read to him, her voice soft but unwavering, full of conviction. She had a scripture for every occasion, a biblical balm for every wound.

Alex reached for the Bible, its pages well-thumbed and annotated in his grandmother's elegant script. He let the book fall open, as if leaving it to fate to speak to him. His eyes fell on Isaiah 41:10, "So do not fear, for I am with you; do not be dismayed, for I am your God. I will strengthen you and help you; I will uphold you with my righteous right hand."

The words were a soothing balm, but his faith was a flickering flame, starved of oxygen and struggling to stay alight. "God, if you're there, if you're really with me," Alex whispered, "show me a sign. Help me understand why this is happening to me."

There was no answer, just the soft sigh of the wind against his window, but somehow, it felt like a response — a gentle nudge reminding him that he was not completely alone.

Alex closed the Bible and placed it back on the nightstand. He knew the road ahead was long and fraught with uncertainty. The whispers of the past were both a comfort and a curse, but they also served as a reminder that he had once been happy, that he had once felt loved.

Sleep eventually claimed him, and for a few hours, he was free from the invisible lines that separated him from the rest of the world. In his dreams, he walked through the hallways not as a ghost, but as just another student, his laughter mingling with that of his peers.

When morning light crept through the blinds, casting a lattice of shadows across his room, Alex awoke with a sense of something shifting within him. It was subtle, like the turn of a page, but it was there — a feeling that maybe, just maybe, he was on the cusp of something new. He got out of bed, a quiet determination settling in his bones, ready to face another day.

Chapter 4: The Echoes of Silence

Alex's school day trudged by with the usual blur of indistinct faces and inaudible conversations. The cafeteria's boisterous energy, a cacophony to some, was to Alex an echo chamber amplifying his solitude. He sat at the edge of the room, his lunch untouched, while the laughter and banter of his classmates swirled around him like a foreign language he couldn't comprehend.

In the noise, he sought refuge in his thoughts, but even there, the echoes of silence were deafening. Alex remembered a time when the silence was comforting, when it was a canvas for his imagination and not a reminder of his isolation. Now, it was just a void, expansive and empty.

Later, in the library, he found solace among the shelves of books, the scent of aged paper a familiar balm. It was one of the few places where the silence felt right, where it was supposed to be, where it enveloped him like a cloak rather than a chain. Here, in the quiet, he could almost feel like himself again.

Alex pulled a Bible from the shelf, the words of the authors speaking to him across time, their voices reaching out from the past to whisper that he wasn't alone in his feelings. There was solace in knowing that centuries ago, someone else had felt this same aching solitude and had transformed it into something beautiful.

Scripture came to mind as he read, the verse from Ecclesiastes 3:1, "There is a time for everything, and a season for every activity under the heavens." It made him ponder the seasons of his own life — this current season of silence and whether it would ever give way to a season of joy.

In the library, Alex's fingers traced the spines of books as if they were the ridges of a well-worn map, each title a destination of escape. The musty air filled his lungs, a mix of paper and possibility. Here, amidst the whisper of turning pages and the soft footsteps of knowledge seekers, he felt a semblance of peace. It was as if the library's quietness spoke a language only he understood, one that whispered, "You are not alone."

He stumbled upon a collection of verses that spoke of resilience in the face of despair, of finding strength in one's own spirit. The words of the authors, long gone, seemed to reach out to him, offering comfort. It was a connection that spanned the chasm of time, a silent communion with souls he'd never met, who had nevertheless laid bare their own sorrows in ink and parchment.

Alex's mind meandered to the biblical story of Elijah, who, after a great victory, had found himself alone and desolate in the wilderness. In 1 Kings 19:12, after a great and powerful wind, after an earthquake, after a fire, God spoke to Elijah in a gentle whisper. This tale resonated with Alex, reminding him that even prophets had known the depths of despair and the feeling of being forsaken.

Each time the library's door opened, spilling noise from the outside world into his refuge, Alex flinched, not ready to leave the cocoon of silence he'd wrapped around himself. But time, relentless in its march, waited for no one. As the hands of the clock inched toward the end of the hour, he felt the familiar tendrils of anxiety creeping up, threatening to pull him back into the sea of noise and eyes that looked past him.

With a heavy heart, he closed the Bible, the echo of the author's voices still ringing in his ears, a stark contrast to the echo of silence that would soon envelop him again. He wondered if there was a verse in the Bible that could encapsulate this moment, this feeling of standing on the precipice between solace and chaos.

Then he remembered, almost as if it was whispered to him, Romans 8:28: "And we know that in all things God works for the good of those who love him, who have been called according to his purpose." It was a promise of purpose amidst chaos, of a plan greater than his pain. It was a difficult verse to hold onto, especially when his current reality seemed so devoid of any plan at all.

Nonetheless, as Alex stepped out of the library, he carried with him the faint echo of hope that had been stirred within the silent symphony of his solitude. Maybe, just maybe, this season of silence was not empty after all, but a preparation for something greater, a prelude to a future where his voice would find its own echo in the world.

Chapter 5: The Unexpected Visitor

The room was heavy with despair, the air thick with the kind of palpable, pressing darkness that seemed to echo Alex's turmoil. He sat on the edge of his bed, a lone figure framed by the ambient light that seeped through the edges of drawn curtains. The crumpled note in his hand was lined with words that spoke of a soul in agony, a silent plea for understanding from a world that had turned its back on him.

Outside, the world slept in blissful ignorance, while inside, Alex's mind was a tempest of destructive thoughts. The silence of his room was a stark contrast to the screaming void within him, a chasm filled with echoes of loneliness and pain. The small pile of pills lay haphazardly on the bedside table, their promise of escape almost tangible. He had reached the end of his tether, and the idea of numbing it all, possibly forever, was the only sliver of 'peace' he could envision.

Alfred Schneider © 2023

As he reached for the drugs, his hand trembling with a cocktail of fear and anticipation, the stillness was abruptly shattered. The door to his room creaked open slowly, as if hesitant, and a figure stepped into the dimness.

At first, Alex's mind refused to accept the presence of another person; it seemed too surreal, too impossible. The man before him had an ordinary appearance, yet something about him was undeniably compelling. His eyes were kind, holding a depth that seemed to span ages, and his voice, when he spoke, was both gentle and authoritative.

He introduced himself as Jesus, and the claim seemed ludicrous, but there was an earnestness in his demeanor that challenged Alex's skepticism. This man, who had seemingly appeared from nowhere, spoke of things no stranger could know. He talked about the dark thoughts that plagued Alex's mind, the feeling of abandonment that had hollowed out his soul, the desperate longing for oblivion that had brought him to this precipice.

Hebrews 4:15 was quoted softly by the visitor:

"For we do not have a high priest who is unable to empathize with our weaknesses, but we have one who has been tempted in every way, just as we are—yet he did not sin."

a reminder that Jesus himself was no stranger to suffering and temptation, yet he remained sinless. This man who called himself Jesus spoke to Alex's aching heart, insisting that he was not alone, that he was understood, that he was loved beyond measure.

As Alex listened, something within him began to crack. The walls he had built, the barriers to keep others out, started to crumble under the weight of unconditional compassion. With every word, the figure chipped away at Alex's resolve, reminding him of the love that awaited him should he choose to accept it.

The conversation seemed to stretch on for hours, yet no time seemed to pass at all. And when Alex finally broke, his tears flowing freely, his cries a mixture of grief and hope, he felt a hand on his shoulder, steadying him, grounding him, saving him.

Alex instantly felt love—a love so profound and steadfast that it had woven itself into the fabric of Alex's very being. This love was not deterred by the barriers Alex had built around himself; it was not thwarted by the gulf of silence he felt between himself and the world. Through Jesus's words, Alex realized that this love, although at times seemed absent from those around him, it was a love that persisted even when he felt most unworthy of it. It was a love that Romans 8:38-39 promised could not be quenched by any force, a love that anchored itself in the deepest part of his soul.

"For I am convinced that neither death nor life, neither angels nor demons, neither the present nor the future, nor any powers, neither height nor depth, nor anything else in all creation, will be able to separate us from the love of God that is in Christ Jesus our Lord."

Jesus, with eyes that seemed to hold the wisdom of the ages, looked deep into Alex's heart and addressed the raw wound of his insignificance. In a world that valued loud voices and visible successes, Alex's quiet existence felt inconsequential. Yet here was Jesus, affirming that Alex's life was precious, that he was seen and known intimately by the Creator. He was reminded of Luke 12:7, where every hair on his head was accounted for, a testament to his value in the eyes of God. This revelation was a balm to the sting of insignificance that had so long plagued his spirit.

And then, with the tenderness of a shepherd guiding his lost sheep, Jesus painted a vision of the future—a future where the haze of despair was lifted, revealing a path marked by hope and purpose. Alex was given a promise, like a seed planted in fertile soil, that his life had a direction, a design that was carefully orchestrated by God Himself. Jeremiah 29:11 echoed in the newfound silence of the room,

"For I know the plans I have for you," declares the Lord, "plans to prosper you and not to harm you, plans to give you hope and a future."

a divine whisper that promised a journey from the depths of despair to the heights of a hopeful destiny.

Jesus left as quietly as he had arrived, and yet the room felt transformed. The oppressive weight that had once constricted Alex's chest seemed to dissolve, leaving a space for something new to grow. In its place was a flickering light, the first sparks of a future illuminated by hope and guided by love—a future where every step was part of a grander plan, every moment an opportunity to live out the purpose that was uniquely his own.

As Alex lay down that night, for the first time in what felt like an eternity, his heart was not racing with anxiety, but beating with a rhythm of peace. The shadows in his room no longer whispered threats; instead, they seemed to caress him into a restful sleep. In this sleep, he dreamed not of escape but of living, not of endings but of beginnings—a dream of life as it could be, as it would be, with hope as his compass and love as his anchor.

Chapter 6: The Battle Within

In the quiet of his room, where shadows seemed to play tricks on his mind, Alex was lost in a tumultuous sea of his own thoughts. The voices in his head, once mere whispers of doubt, had now increased into a loudness of despair. They painted his consciousness with images so vivid and cruel, they felt suffocatingly real. His classmates, with their cold, piercing eyes, appeared before him, each one echoing the sentiment of disdain and worthlessness. "You're a waste of space, Alex," one sneered. "Why not just end it all?"

The parade of these harrowing apparitions continued unabated, each one echoing the same relentless message of rejection and insignificance. Teachers, figures of authority and respect in Alex's life, now looked upon him with disappointment and regret. "I wish I never set eyes on you," one of them uttered, sending a chill through Alex's already shaken soul.

However, nothing prepared him for the images of his parents, the people who were supposed to be his sanctuary in a world of chaos. His father's figure, usually a source of strength, now stared back at him with eyes full of scorn.4 "I get depressed every time you're in the same room as me. You're a constant reminder of disappointment," his father's image said, each word a crushing blow to Alex's crumbling self-worth.

Then came the image of his mother, her visage twisting into an expression of regret and disdain. "I regret giving birth to you. You're a loser, and I'm ashamed to call you my son," she said, her words cutting deeper than any physical wound could.

The room seemed to spin around Alex as the voices and images continued their relentless assault. The once comforting silence now echoed with the voices of condemnation and self-loathing, leaving him feeling more isolated than ever. The good voice, once a beacon of hope and reassurance, was now nowhere to be heard, drowned out by the overwhelming tide of despair.

As the night progressed, the images and voices gradually began to wane, leaving Alex in a state of exhausted vulnerability. But just as he thought the worst was over, a new voice emerged, one that he recognized instantly and that had always been a source of comfort and love – his grandmother's voice.

"Alex," the voice called out, seemingly from a distance. A flicker of hope ignited within him. His grandmother had always been his anchor, her words a source of unconditional love and wisdom. But as her image materialized, Alex's fleeting sense of relief was shattered. The loving, kind expression he remembered was replaced by one of indifference and agreement with the tormenting chorus that had preceded her.

"You know, everyone else is right," his grandmother's image said coldly. "No one loves you; no one ever did."

In disbelief, Alex whispered, "No, Grandma, it's not true. I knew what I felt when I was with you. I knew you loved me; this can't be real."

But the image of his grandmother was unyielding. "There was never any true love on my end, Alex. I just tolerated you because no one else did. You should just end it all because no one will care."

Alex felt as if the very ground beneath him was giving way. The tears came then, uncontrollable and bitter, each one a testament to the pain and betrayal he felt. The one person he had always believed loved him unconditionally was now part of the chorus of voices urging him toward despair.

As the night wore on, the images and voices seemed to swirl around him, a relentless storm of negativity and hopelessness. The room, once his sanctuary, now felt like a prison, the walls closing in on him, suffocating him with the weight of his own despair.

He lay there, curled up on the floor, as the hours ticked by, each minute stretching into an eternity of agony. The voices continued their merciless barrage, each word a nail in the coffin of his broken spirit. His mind replayed every moment of rejection, every instance of failure, every word of contempt, over and over, like a broken record that he couldn't turn off.

The idea of escape, of an end to the pain, became a seductive whisper in the back of his mind. But even in his darkest moment, a part of Alex clung desperately to a sliver of rational thought, a faint voice urging him to hold on, to survive the night.

The first light of dawn found Alex still on the floor, physically and emotionally exhausted. The voices had finally quieted, leaving behind a deafening silence. He felt numb, drained of all emotion, a hollow shell of the person he once was.

As the sun rose, casting its light into the room, it brought no comfort to Alex. The new day was not a symbol of hope or a new beginning, but a stark reminder of the relentless passage of time, of the ongoing struggle that awaited him.

In that moment, Alex realized that the battle within him was far from over. The voices might have receded for now, but he knew they would return, perhaps even stronger than before. He was caught in an unending cycle of despair, a prisoner in his own mind, with no clear path to salvation.

Chapter 7: Echoes of Hope

The night had been long, and the morning light seemed to creep slowly into Alex's room, as if hesitant to disturb the remnants of darkness that lingered. The previous night's torment had left Alex in a state of exhausted despair. The room, once filled with the haunting echoes of condemnation, now lay in a profound silence, a canvas waiting for a new painting.

As Alex lay there, his thoughts a tangled web of confusion and pain, he yearned for a glimpse of light, a sign of hope, anything to counter the dreadful weight of desolation that clung to him. He desperately needed to feel that sense of love and peace he once felt, the one that momentarily lifted the veil of darkness from his world.

It was then that he heard it – a voice, the same comforting voice that had spoken to him before. The voice of Jesus. Though he couldn't see Him, the presence in the room was unmistakable, a sense of love and peace that permeated the very air.

"Alex," the voice echoed gently, "the voices and visions that tormented you, they were not real. They were lies planted in your mind by the enemy, designed to deceive and destroy you."

Alex listened, his heart pounding in his chest. Jesus' words offered a stark contrast to the despairing thoughts that had consumed him.

Then, the room seemed to transform, and Alex found himself witnessing scenes from his life, as if watching a movie where he was both the actor and the audience. He saw himself walking down the school hallways, feeling lonely and invisible. But as the scene played out, it gradually shifted – classmates were waving at him, trying to catch his attention; teachers were looking at him with eyes full of concern and pity, hoping to reach out to him.

His confusion deepened. "How could this be, Jesus? None of this ever happened. No one notices me. I'm a nobody."

Jesus' voice was tender, like a father comforting a child. "Alex, these moments are real. Your pain blinded you to the truth around you. Your hurt made you feel invisible, unseen, unloved."

Then Jesus quoted a scripture, a balm to Alex's wounded soul, "You are fearfully and wonderfully made. Your value is immeasurable, and your life is a precious gift."

As the scenes continued, Alex saw himself at home, passing by his parents in the kitchen. But unlike his reality, in these visions, his parents turned towards him, their faces breaking into smiles of genuine love. They ran to him, embracing him, their words a chorus of love and affection, pleading with him to see the truth of their emotions.

Alex's heart ached with confusion and longing. "But why couldn't I see this, Jesus? Why did it all feel like a lie?"

"Your pain clouded your vision, Alex," Jesus replied. "But know this – my love for you is unchanging, unwavering, and unconditional."

Jesus then spoke of His own sacrifice, detailing the pain and suffering He endured on the cross. He described the agony of feeling abandoned by His Father, the betrayal of His disciples, and the weight of the world's sins upon Him. Scripture after scripture confirmed the truth of His words, painting a vivid picture of the ultimate act of love.

"And yet, I rose on the third day," Jesus continued. "I overcame death, not just for the sake of victory, but out of love for you, Alex. My resurrection was a testament to the boundless, unfathomable love I have for you."

The room was filled with an overwhelming sense of love and sacrifice, touching the very core of Alex's being. But there was more. Jesus reminded him of his grandmother, her unwavering faith, and her nightly prayers for Alex's well-being.

"Your grandmother loved you deeply, Alex. Her prayers were for your protection, for your happiness. She always asked Me to watch over you, to remind you in your darkest moments that everything will be alright if you just cling to Me."

The memories of his grandmother, her love and her prayers, brought a sense of warmth and comfort to Alex's heart. It was a stark contrast to the cold, despairing thoughts that had plagued him.

As the day wore on, the words and visions that Jesus shared with Alex began to take root in his heart. The weight of despair started to lift, replaced by a budding sense of hope and an emerging belief in the love that surrounded him – both divine and earthly.

That night, as Alex lay in his bed, the echoes of hope resonated within him. The words of Jesus, the reminders of his grandmother's love, and the newfound realization of his worth and the care of those around him intertwined, forming a shield against the lies of the enemy.

Alfred Schneider © 2023

For the first time in a long while, Alex drifted off to sleep, not with thoughts of despair and loneliness, but with a heart beginning to be filled with the echoes of hope, a hope that whispered of better days, of love and life worth living. The chapter closed, not on a note of despair, but with a gentle, burgeoning promise that the darkest night would eventually give way to the dawn of a new day, filled with love and light.

Chapter 8: Unseen Bonds

In the soft light of the morning, Alex awoke with a sense of purpose he hadn't felt in a long time. The echoes of hope that had begun to resonate within him the previous day had set a change in motion, a shift in perspective that now urged him to reach out, to reconnect with the world he had felt so detached from.

The thought of reaching out to his family and friends, after months of feeling invisible and disconnected, filled Alex with a mixture of anxiety and a burgeoning sense of hope. His recent revelations had opened his eyes to a different reality – one where he was seen, heard, and loved.

With a deep breath, Alex picked up his phone. The first call he made was to his cousin, Lily, who had always been more like a sister to him. He had distanced himself from her during his months of despair, ignoring her calls and messages.

"Alex? Is that really you?" Lily's voice was a mixture of surprise and delight.

"I've been so worried about you. We all have."

Alex's heart clenched at her words. "I'm sorry, Lily. I... I've been going through a lot."

Lily's response was immediate and heartfelt. "Alex, you don't have to go through anything alone. We're here for you, always. I just wish I could've done more to help."

The conversation with Lily set the tone for the rest of the day. Alex reached out to friends he had pushed away, each call revealing the same truth – they had seen him all along, had cared for him, and had wished they could break through the walls he had built around himself.

His friend Mark expressed relief and happiness upon hearing from Alex. "Man, I've missed you. I've been trying to get your attention at school, but you seemed so lost in your own world. I just didn't know how to help."

Hearing these words, seeing the truth in them, was both heartwarming and overwhelming for Alex. For so long, he had been convinced of his invisibility, of his insignificance. But now, each voice on the other end of the line painted a different picture – one of concern, of missed connections, and of unspoken prayers for his wellbeing.

At home, the change in Alex's perception was even more profound. His parents, whom he had believed indifferent to his existence, were overjoyed by his newfound willingness to engage. They embraced him, tears of relief and love in their eyes.

His mother held him close, kissing his forehead. "My baby boy, we've been so worried about you. Your father and I... we've been praying every night, hoping you would come to us, let us help."

His father, a man of few words, expressed his feelings with a firm, reassuring embrace. "Son, we're here for you, always. No matter what you're going through, you're not alone."

Alex was stunned. The stark contrast between his perceived reality and the genuine affection his parents showed him was almost too much to bear. For months, he had been trapped in a world of his own making, a world where he was invisible and unloved. But now, the truth was laid bare – his family and friends had always cared, had always seen him, even when he couldn't see himself.

The day was filled with revelations and emotional reunions. Each interaction, each expression of concern and love, chipped away at the walls Alex had built around himself. The feeling of being invisible, of being alone, was slowly being replaced by a sense of belonging, of being an integral part of a larger whole.

Yet, despite the overwhelming evidence of love and concern, Alex found it hard to completely let go of the doubts that had been his constant companions for so long. The months of isolation and despair had left deep scars, and part of him still struggled to accept this newfound reality.

As night fell, Alex lay in bed, reflecting on the day's events. The voices of his family and friends echoed in his mind, each word a testament to their love and concern. Yet, a small part of him still hesitated, still doubted.

But amidst the whirlwind of emotions, there was a glimmer of hope, a willingness to believe in this new reality, to embrace the love that had always been there but had been obscured by his own pain and despair.

As Alex drifted off to sleep, he made a silent promise to himself – to try, to keep reaching out, to allow himself to be seen and heard. He didn't know what the future held, but for the first time in a long time, he was willing to find out, to step out of the shadows and into the light.

Chapter 9: The Silent Strength

Alex woke up to a new day, a day that seemed like any other, yet something within him had shifted. The previous day's revelations had brought a sense of hope and belonging, a feeling he hadn't experienced in a long time. However, as the morning sun streamed through his window, casting a warm glow across his room, the familiar pangs of doubt and uncertainty began to resurface.

Sitting at the edge of his bed, Alex's mind was a tumultuous sea of questions. Were the expressions of love and concern from his family and friends genuine? Did they truly mean what they said about wishing they could do more? These questions, like insidious whispers, began to weave a web of uncertainty around his heart.

As he went about his day, the questions continued to haunt him. Every smile, every kind word from those around him, was scrutinized under the lens of his doubts. The feeling of being invisible, which he thought he had begun to shake off, crept back, casting a shadow over the newfound light in his life.

But amidst this turmoil, something remarkable happened. As the questions and doubts swirled in his mind, a sudden surge of courage welled up within him. With a newfound resolve, Alex began to speak aloud to himself, affirming his worth and value.

He started quoting scriptures, the words flowing from him like a soothing balm to his troubled soul. "I am fearfully and wonderfully made," he declared, the words echoing around his room, filling the space with a sense of purpose and strength.

Alex continued, his voice growing more confident with each verse. "For God so loved the world, that He gave His only Son, that whoever believes in Him should not perish but have eternal life." The scripture reminded him of the immense love Jesus had for him, a love so profound that it led to the ultimate sacrifice on the cross of Calvary.

As he spoke these words of affirmation, Alex felt the negative thoughts receding, as if they were being physically pushed out of his mind. He could almost hear them screaming in frustration, "No, it can't be, we didn't win."

A sense of pride swelled within Alex. He realized that he, alongside Jesus, had the power to overcome any negativity that tried to infiltrate his mind. The realization that he was not powerless against his thoughts, that he had the strength and the support to combat them, was liberating.

With this new understanding, Alex felt a shift in his perception. He began to see his interactions with his family and friends in a new light. The love and concern they expressed no longer seemed questionable. Instead, they were like threads weaving a safety net of support and understanding around him.

As the day turned into evening, Alex found himself reflecting on the journey he had embarked upon. He understood now that the path to healing was not linear, that there would be days filled with doubts and fears. But he also knew that he had the tools to confront these challenges, to silence the whispers of uncertainty with the loud, resonant voice of faith and love.

He remembered a scripture that had always given him strength, "I can do all things through Christ who strengthens me." This verse was a reminder that his strength did not come from himself alone, but from a higher power, from a love that was eternal and unwavering.

As he lay in bed that night, Alex felt a sense of peace enveloping him. He knew that the journey ahead would have its share of obstacles, but he also knew that he was no longer alone in facing them. With Jesus by his side, and the assurance of the love of his family and friends, the negative thoughts and feelings that once seemed insurmountable were now just hurdles he was equipped to overcome.

Chapter 10: Whispers of Change

As the soft hues of dawn broke through the horizon, marking the beginning of a new day, there was an undeniable change in the air. It was a change that resonated deeply within Alex, a transformation that had gradually taken root and was now in full bloom. This new day was not just another sequence of hours; it was a testament to a new beginning, a new Alex.

Gone were the days of isolation and despair, the days when Alex felt invisible and unloved. The Alex that greeted this day was one filled with joy, hope, and an eagerness to be around people. He was like a flower that had finally opened up to the sunlight after a long, harsh winter.

As he prepared for the day, Alex found himself humming a tune, a melody that seemed to spring from the newfound joy in his heart. Every reflection in the mirror showed a face that was brighter, eyes that sparkled with life, and a smile that was genuine and full of warmth.

Alfred Schneider © 2023

At school, the change in Alex was evident to everyone. Where once he walked the halls with his head down, lost in a world of his own, he now moved with a confident stride, greeting classmates with a smile and a kind word. The transformation was so profound that it didn't just affect Alex; it created ripples around him, touching the lives of those he interacted with.

In every opportunity he had, Alex shared his extraordinary encounter with Jesus. He spoke of the darkness that had once enveloped him, the vivid images and voices that whispered of his insignificance and invisibility. But more importantly, he spoke of the overpowering love of Jesus that had shattered those illusions, showing him the truth.

He recounted how Jesus had revealed to him the genuine concerns and prayers of those around him, dispelling his darkest fears and replacing them with an undeniable reality of love and care. His story, raw and honest, touched the hearts of those who listened, offering hope and inspiring faith.

In the classroom, Alex's newfound enthusiasm for life was infectious. He participated in discussions with a zeal that was both refreshing and inspiring. Teachers, who had once worried about his withdrawn nature, now marveled at the remarkable turnaround.

Even during lunchtime, a time he used to dread, Alex found joy in the company of others. He joined his classmates, engaging in conversations, sharing laughs, and forging new friendships. The loneliness that had once consumed him was now replaced by a sense of belonging and community.

After school, Alex volunteered at a local community center, a place where he felt he could give back some of the love and hope he had received. He worked with children, helping them with their homework and playing games with them, his heart swelling with happiness at every smile he brought to their faces.

In these interactions, Alex found a deeper purpose. He realized that his journey, his transformation, could be a source of inspiration to others. He talked to the children about the importance of hope, about believing in themselves, and about the power of love to overcome any obstacle.

Back at home, the change in Alex brought a new sense of harmony and joy. His parents, who had once been worried and distant, now found new ways to connect with their son. They shared meals, talked about their days, and laughed together – a family united by love and strengthened by the trials they had overcome.

Each night, as he lay in bed, Alex reflected on the day's events with a heart full of gratitude. He thought about the smiles he had shared, the stories he had told, and the lives he had touched. He realized that his transformation was not just about him; it was a beacon of hope for others, a living testimony to the power of faith and love.

The whispers of change that had begun as a faint murmur in Alex's heart were now a loud, resounding chorus. A chorus that sang of hope, of transformation, and of the unyielding power of love to conquer the deepest darkness. Alex had emerged not just as a survivor, but as a beacon of light, an embodiment of the change that is possible when love and faith take the lead.

Chapter 11: Mending Bridges

The early rays of the morning sunbathed Alex's room in a soft, warm light, heralding the start of another day. But for Alex, each day was more than just a sequence of hours; it was an opportunity to share the remarkable transformation he had experienced. The burden of unworthiness and invisibility that had once shackled him now seemed like a distant memory, replaced by a relentless drive to spread the message of hope and love he had received.

As he prepared for the day, Alex reflected on his journey. He remembered vividly the endless nights of despair, the constant battle with the negative voice in his head that told him he was unloved and unworthy. But then, there was that pivotal moment - the unexpected visit from Jesus, the turning point in his life.

Alfred Schneider © 2023

Everywhere Alex went, he shared his story, his voice imbued with passion and conviction. He spoke to anyone who would listen, recounting how Jesus had appeared to him during his darkest hour, showing him the way, the truth, and the life. He described how Jesus had opened his eyes, revealing that the darkness blinding him was a product of his own pain and hurt.

Alex's story resonated with many, touching the hearts of those who had known their own struggles with feeling invisible and unloved. He quoted scripture, his words echoing with the power of transformation. "Therefore, if anyone is in Christ, he is a new creation; the old has gone, the new has come!" he would proclaim, his eyes shining with the joy of his newfound faith.

His journey of mending bridges began with his own family. Alex

spent time with his parents, sharing his experiences and the profound change in his perspective.
He expressed his gratitude for their unwavering love, even when he couldn't see it. His parents, moved by his words and transformation, found a deeper connection with their son, one founded on mutual understanding and renewed love.

Alex's friends, too, witnessed a change in him. He reached out, mending relationships that had frayed during his time of isolation. His openness and newfound joy were infectious, drawing his friends closer and inspiring them with his story of transformation.

Chapter 12 : The Invisible Made Visible

As Alex continued to share his story, he realized that his transformation was not just about himself. It was about making the invisible visible, about shining a light in the darkness for others to find their way. He became involved in community projects, speaking at schools, and participating in church activities, always eager to share the message of hope and love.

He spoke about the importance of recognizing the struggles of those who felt invisible, of extending a hand to those in need. His words were a call to action, inspiring others to look beyond their own experiences and to reach out with empathy and understanding.

Alex's message was one of empowerment and hope. He

encouraged people to seek their own transformations, to open their hearts to the possibility of renewal in Christ. He became a living testimony to the power of faith, a beacon of light in his community, guiding others towards a path of healing and love.

The early morning light filtered through the curtains of Alex's room, casting a serene glow that felt like a soft embrace. As he lay in bed, his mind wandered back to the journey he had embarked upon – a journey that had transformed him from a prisoner of despair to a beacon of hope. The verses from 2 Corinthians 5:17 echoed in his heart, "Therefore, if anyone is in Christ, the new creation has come: The old has gone, the new is here!" This verse was a testament to the profound change he had experienced.

Rising from his bed, Alex felt a sense of purpose pulsing through him. The days of feeling invisible were behind him; he had emerged as a visible testament to the transformative power of faith and love. As he prepared for the day, he remembered the words of Jesus in Matthew 5:14, "You are the light of the world. A town built on a hill cannot be hidden." This verse reminded him of his responsibility to shine his light, to guide others out of their shadows of despair.

At school, Alex's transformation was not just visible in his demeanor but also in his interactions. Where once he had shield away from his peers, he now approached them with a gentle confidence, offering a listening ear and a compassionate heart. His conversations were often sprinkled with words of encouragement, drawing from the well of Scripture that had become his source of strength. He frequently shared Psalm 34:18, "The Lord is close to the brokenhearted and saves those who are crushed in spirit," as a balm for those struggling around him.

Alex's commitment extended beyond the school walls. He volunteered at a local youth center, sharing his story and the hope he found in Christ. His words were a tapestry woven with the threads of his own experiences, each story a patch in the quilt of his testimony. He often reflected on Romans 8:28, "And we know that in all things God works for the good of those who love him, who have been called according to his purpose." This verse underpinned his belief that every challenge he faced

Alfred Schneider © 2023

was a step towards fulfilling God's purpose for him.

As days turned into weeks, Alex's influence grew. He started a small group for students at his school, a safe space where they could share their struggles and find solace in the Word of God. He found joy in facilitating discussions, often turning to Philippians 4:6-7, "Do not be anxious about anything, but in every situation, by prayer and petition, with thanksgiving, present your requests to God." This passage was a cornerstone of their meetings, reminding everyone to seek peace through prayer.

One evening, as he walked home under the starlit sky, Alex pondered over the parable of the Lost Sheep in Luke 15:4-6. He realized that like the shepherd who rejoiced over finding one lost sheep, his efforts, no matter how small, made a difference in God's eyes. This realization filled him with a profound sense of purpose and gratitude.

Alex's journey had become more than just a personal transformation; it was a testament to the invisible made visible to the power of faith in revealing the unseen. He had become a vessel of hope, a living echo of God's love, resonating in the hearts of those he touched. As he looked up at the vast expanse of the night sky, he whispered a prayer of thanks, knowing that in this vast universe, he had found his place, his voice, and his purpose.

Chapter 13 : A Journey of Faith

Alex's journey had now become a journey of faith, a daily walk in the light of the love he had received. He found joy in every interaction, every opportunity to share his story and the message of Jesus' love. He continued to quote scriptures, each verse a reminder of the transformative power of faith.

He spoke of the sacrifice of Jesus on the cross, of the love so profound that it overcame death and offered salvation to all. Alex's words were not just stories; they were invitations to experience a love and joy that transcended all understanding, a peace that only Jesus could give.

As he moved through his days, Alex's faith deepened. He spent time in prayer and meditation, seeking guidance and wisdom in his journey. He found solace and strength in his relationship with Christ, a relationship that had become the cornerstone of his life.

One day, as he was reading his Bible, a particular passage stood out to him: "Go into all the world and preach the gospel to all creation" (Mark 16:15). Alex felt a stirring in his heart, a call to share his story more broadly. He knew what he had to do. He decided to go to the marketplace to speak to everyone about his experience with Jesus.

The next Saturday, Alex arrived at the bustling marketplace, filled with vibrant colors of fresh produce and the lively chatter of people. He set up a makeshift platform—a simple crate—and stood with his Bible in hand, his heart pounding with anticipation and a touch of nervousness.

Taking a deep breath, he began, "Listen, everyone," his voice cutting through the ambient noise and drawing curious glances from the crowd. "I know it might seem out of the ordinary for me to speak up like this, but I believe it's no coincidence that you are all here today. Something far greater has led me to this moment, to tell you about a change so deep, it has redefined my entire existence."

He paused, ensuring he had their attention, then continued, "There was a time when I felt utterly invisible, swallowed by a sea of faces, each day a struggle against a tide of loneliness and despair. The pain was suffocating, pushing me to the brink where I saw no worth in continuing. But in my darkest moment, when hope seemed like a distant memory, I had an encounter that changed everything."

Alfred Schneider © 2023

"The person I met was no ordinary figure. He was Jesus. And before you dismiss this as mere religious speak, let me share how this encounter wasn't just spiritual—it was transformational. Jesus showed me that despite my feelings of insignificance, I was seen, known, and deeply loved. He revealed to me a perspective where every moment of suffering had a purpose, even if I couldn't see it at the time."

"Jesus's love and the sacrifice he made on the cross wasn't just for me—it's for you as well. His journey to Calvary wasn't just a passage through pain but a profound demonstration of unconditional love. This love has the power to transform, to heal, to uplift from despair. And I stand here today, a living testament to that transformative power."

"I tell you this not to convert you on the spot or to claim that my path should be yours. No, I share this because in the heart of this market, amidst your daily routines, there is a message of hope and renewal waiting for you. It's not by chance that you're hearing this; it's a divine moment of interruption, meant to stir something within you."

"So, take a moment, reflect on where you stand in life. If there's a void, a shadow, or a whisper of doubt about your worth and purpose, know that there is a way through. I found my path through Jesus, and perhaps, just maybe, there's a message in my story for you too."

As Alex concluded, the air seemed charged with a new energy. Faces that had shown skepticism now reflected contemplation. He didn't expect everyone to accept what he said, but if it planted a seed of hope in even one heart, then sharing his

Alfred Schneider © 2023

journey was worth every moment of vulnerability.

After he stepped down from the crate, a man approached him. He looked deeply moved, with tears in his eyes. "What you said... it touched me," he confessed. "I've been struggling, feeling lost. Hearing your story gives me hope."

Alex smiled, feeling the warmth of the man's words. "I'm glad it helped," he replied. "Remember, you're not alone. There's always hope, and there's always love to be found."

In the days that followed, word of Alex's testimony spread. More people approached him, curious and seeking the same hope and transformation he had found. Alex realized that his journey was far from over; it was just beginning. The marketplace had become a new

Alfred Schneider © 2023

chapter in his story, a place where he could share his faith and bring light to those in darkness.

One evening, as Alex was reflecting on the day's events, he received a message from Sarah Goodwill. She wanted to meet and talk about his experience. They arranged to meet at a local coffee shop.

The air was crisp, and the sun was setting, casting long shadows on the sidewalk as Alex walked to the coffee shop. When he arrived, he saw Sarah sitting at a corner table, a look of intense curiosity on her face. Next to her was Detective Michael Andrews, who had a serious and focused demeanor.

Alex approached the table, feeling a mix of anticipation and unease. Sarah looked up and smiled warmly as he reached them. "Alex?"

she asked, her tone both welcoming and uncertain.

"Yes, that's me," Alex replied, taking a seat. "And you must be Sarah. It's nice to meet you."

Sarah nodded, glancing briefly at Michael before continuing. "Thank you for coming. This is Detective Michael Andrews, a family friend and investigator helping me with... well, a very personal matter."

Michael offered a brief nod. "Nice to meet you, Alex."

Sarah leaned forward, her expression earnest. "I wanted to ask if you're the same Alex who spoke at the marketplace a few weeks ago. Your testimony about your encounter with Jesus—it deeply moved my father, Pastor John Goodwill. Was that you?"

Alex felt a surge of recognition and nodded. "Yes, that was me. I'm glad my story touched him. How is Pastor John?"

Sarah's face clouded with concern. "That's why we wanted to meet with you. My father has gone missing. He left behind a letter, and ever since Detective Andrews and I started following the clues in the letter, I've been receiving these threatening notes."

Alex's brow furrowed. "Threatening notes? What kind of notes?"

Sarah reached into her bag and pulled out a small, crumpled piece of paper. She handed it to Alex. "This is the latest one I received: 'Consider this a friendly caution: Continue this quest at your own peril.'"

Alex read the note, feeling a chill run down his spine. He looked up, meeting Sarah's eyes. "This is serious. Do you think it has something to do with your father's disappearance?"

Sarah nodded, her eyes filled with worry. "I do. My father was deeply moved by your story. He was exploring new ideas, questioning things he had always believed. I think he found something—or someone— he wasn't supposed to."

Michael leaned in, his voice low and steady. "We've been following the clues in Pastor John's letter, but it's led us into dangerous territory. We need your help, Alex. You might know something that can help us find him."

Alex took a deep breath, realizing the gravity of the situation. "I'll do whatever I can to help. Your father was seeking the truth, just like I was. Maybe together, we can uncover what happened to him."

Sarah gave him a grateful smile. "Thank you, Alex. We need all the help we can get. My father always believed in the power of faith and truth. We have to find him and understand what he was trying to uncover."

Alex nodded, feeling a deep sense of responsibility. "Let's do it. Let's find your father and get to the bottom of this."

As they sat in the coffee shop, discussing the next steps, Alex couldn't shake the feeling that this meeting was more significant than it seemed. He glanced at the note again, feeling the weight of the words. Whatever lay ahead, it was going to change everything.

Chapter 14 : A Message from the Author

As the author of this book, I find myself reflecting on the journey that has led to these pages – a journey that mirrors the one taken by Alex, our protagonist. This story, while a work of fiction, is deeply rooted in the truths of my own life as a young man. It is a tale born from personal struggles, from battles fought in the silence of the soul, and from the transformative power of faith and redemption.

Growing up, I was different from my peers, which made fitting in a constant struggle. This sense of being an outsider was compounded by feelings of invisibility, of being unloved and insecure. Like Alex, I grappled with these intense emotions, feeling a profound disconnect from the world around me. The struggle to find hope in the midst of despair was a daily battle, one that often left me feeling defeated and alone.

My journey as a Christian wasn't straightforward either. There were moments when I felt abandoned by God, times when my faith wavered under the weight of loneliness and doubt. The voices urging self-destruction, though different in method from those that haunted Alex, were just as real and just as insidious. They whispered of sharp objects, of oncoming cars, of over-the-counter medications – each suggestion a sinister echo of my inner turmoil.

But, like Alex, my life was profoundly changed by an unexpected encounter with Jesus Christ. It happened one Friday evening, a time when my struggles were known only to me. During a seemingly ordinary conversation at church, a friend, moved to tears, shared a divine message that struck at the very core of my being.

"I can feel your pain, AJ," she said. "God has heard your cries, you're longing for a friend, your silent prayers from your window." Her words were a direct response to my private pleas, a moment of divine intervention that revealed God's intimate awareness of my struggles.

That experience marked a turning point in my life. It shifted my perspective and transformed my relationship with God. Jesus became more than a figure of faith; He became a friend, a confidant, a constant presence in my life. In times of sadness and loneliness, I turned to Him. In moments of joy and triumph, He was the first to hear my praise.

This book was written to share that transformation with you, the reader. If God could reach into the depths of my despair and bring forth joy, He is more than capable of doing the same for you. His love is unfathomable, so great that He gave His only Son, Jesus, to die for us, as John 3:16 so beautifully states: "For God so loved the world that He gave His one and only Son, that whoever believes in Him shall not perish but have eternal life."

If you have stumbled upon this book, or if it was recommended to you, know that it is not a coincidence. It is a divine appointment, an opportunity for you to hear the resounding message of God's love. He sees you, He hears you, and He speaks to you now: "My dear child, I love you. I have never forsaken you. I have been with you all the days of your life and will never leave you."

Alfred Schneider © 2023

Dear Lord Jesus,

I come to You today recognizing that I am a sinner in need of Your grace and forgiveness. I acknowledge that I cannot save myself and that my efforts are not enough. I believe that You died on the cross for my sins and rose again, offering me new life and hope.

I confess my sins to You and ask for Your forgiveness. Please cleanse me and make me new. I open my heart to You and invite You to come in. Be my Lord and Savior. Guide my life and help me to follow You.

Thank You, Jesus, for Your love and sacrifice. Thank You for giving me eternal life and for the promise of being with You forever. From this day forward, I am Yours, and I place my trust in You.

In Jesus' Name,

Amen.

Made in United States
Orlando, FL
15 July 2024

49004963R00049